THE CHATEAUX DE LA LOIRE

Introduction by
ANDRÉ CASTELOT

Text by

JANINE ET PIERRE SOISSON
Translated by David MaCrae

MINERVA

How is one to account for the fascination French royalty always felt for the regions of Orléanais, Blésois, Touraine and Anjou? Part of the answer is security. The king was thus able to be far from frontiers which enemies frequently crossed; he was also able to govern the country from its geographical center; lastly, and particularly, on the banks of the royal river, the sovereign felt that he was in touch with the heartbeat of the real France. The harmony, the serene beauty and the soft line of the landscape, its blond sands, light willows and shimmering poplars were—and still are—an expression of the grace, taste and sense of measure which are the quintessential French qualities. The Loire Valley can truly be said to be the core of the country.

It is said that the Normans went up the river, but had no time to land, and no foreign influence thus sullied the purity of the region's race and, more particularly, of its language. Boileau once said that he wished all Frenchmen were able to speak their language "like the stevedores unloading hay on the wharves in Paris, men who were virtually all natives of the Loire Valley. And today the inhabitants of the valley—the *Vallards* of Orléannais, *Varenniers* of Blésois or Touraine, the *Valléiais* of Anjou—still speak a very pure French.

Early in the 15th century— about the time when Charles VII made his first appearance on the banks of the Loire—the quadrangular keeps of the late 10th and the 11th centuries, such as those of Montrichard, Beaugency or Montbazon, were no longer used as residences. The royal dwellings, the château of Chinon and especially that of Saumur, were perceived in a way which we can hardly imagine today. It is still possible to see in the *Riches Heures* of the duke of Berry the château of Saumur as a traveler arriving from the vine-covered hillocks would have seen it. Behind a powerful defensive system—corner towers in semi-circles, low towers become broader towards the moats—there stood an imposing array of slender white towers of a Gothic residence.

Renaissance influences eventually caused brick to be supplanted by an emphasis on fine-patterned stonework. Outside the towns, the châteaux moved down into the valleys. Instead of the stagnant moats of the past, the mansions were now reflected in the rivers; indeed, some of them were built astride the waterway itself. Warlike trappings were kept, but only to let travelers know that they were passing the residence of a noble.

The "château of the Loire" style culminated at Chambord in a dazzling display of fireworks in stone.

In the words of Maurice Bedel, "from one bank of the Loire to the other, the centuries exchange memories".

Every hillock thus reminds us of a scene, a word or a gesture. How precious it is to be able to say:

"It was here, and nothing has moved!"

We should feel sorry for those who scorn this sentimental reaction, as they are denying themselves a great joy.

ANDRÉ CASTELOT

The splendid Très Riches Heures du Duc de Berry, *the most famous of the medieval illuminated manuscripts, contains many descriptions of life about the time when the first of* the great châteaux were built. Here are two examples. A little further on, the château of Saumur, as depicted in the manuscript.

"Along the gently curving hillocks and the noble valleys, the châteaux are strewn like so many resting places, and in the majesty of mornings and evenings the Loire and its vassals move sedately along these paths, while one hundred and twenty châteaux pay hommage".

This was how Charles Péguy saw the magnificent Loire Valley, with its tender and bright sky and its harmonious landscape—a region which has produced, in its own image, the most refined and aristocratic art of France.

The Loire can be said to have formed the historical backbone of the kingdom of France during the Middle Ages and the 16th century. It marks the rough boundary between the *langue d'oc* and the *langue d'oil*. During the 15th century, throughout the Hundred Years' War involving English, French, Burgundians and Armagnacs, and which set the seal on national unity, military success or failure at crucial moments often depended on actions in the Loire Valley. Hence the region's incomparable historical importance, which was to be accompanied by a splendid cultural wealth.

From the year 1000 onwards, sanctuaries began to be built in Orléanais, Touraine and Anjou, very much in the Romanesque style.

The regions' architecture changed in the second half of the 12th century, and the Anjou style, sometimes known as Plantagenet (on account of Henry II of England, the husband of Eléonore of Aquitaine) then emerged as a transitional style which reached its apex in the 13th century, and then faded quite abruptly. It was supplanted by the Gothic period, and in particular by Flamboyant Gothic, which is to be found in the Abbey of the Trinity (Vendôme), Saint-Gatien (Tours) and Notre-Dame de Cléry.

The Loire Valley was to be the setting for the emergence, under a variety of influences, of the most elegant French art and of a series of buildings which soon became a part of French folklore: "Orléans, Beaugency, Notre-Dame de Cléry, Vendôme...".

Some extraordinary gems of architecture were created on the banks of the Loire during the Renaissance: they are what we understand by the term "Châteaux of the Loire".

With the invention of gunpowder and advances in artillery, the old medieval fortress began to crumble away. The Hundred Years' War had already shown the importance of infantry, the new queen of the battlefield, and the decline of cavalry. These trends became accentuated during the 16th century, as artillery and infantry assumed decisive importance in military engagements. War became a matter of movement, with sieges as the exception. The fortress had outlived its usefulness; just after the first expeditions of Charles VIII in Italy, the French nobility, who had had a chance to savor for themselves the architectural charms of the peninsula, began either to alter their fortresses, or to construct new châteaux with a new purpose in mind: not defense, but comfort and elegance at home. There could hardly have been a more suitable place for this to happen. The lower reaches of the Loire are blessed with a gentle climate and an incomparable charm. The meandering course of the only river situated entirely inside French territory proceeds through a serene landscape, calmly flowing through a rich and fertile land of vineyards and orchards. It is therefore only natural that the Loire Valley has been chosen as a showcase of architectural and artistic beauty at a time when France is taking a renewed interest in its heritage.

Louis XI heralded the 16th century by bringing from Italy artists such as Francesco Laurano, Nicollo Spinelli, Jean Candida and others. The last king of the Middle Ages was already moving away from the stern walls of the old Louvre, and making the château of Plessis-lès-Tours his favorite residence. Long before the Renaissance itself, Italian influence thus made its appearance in France. It really started to thrive when Charles VIII, at the end of 1495, returned from

Naples with a legion of artists who brought rich new blood to French art. Fortresses were turned into luxurious residences. Amboise, Chaumont, and even Chenonceau, Azay and Chambord kept something of a fortress-like air, though their battlements were little more than decorative touches. The façades were adorned with medallions and low reliefs. The simpler openings of an earlier were replaced by wide bays framed by pilasters, and the rooftops now bristled with sculpted chimneys. The excessive brilliance of the imported Italian style was soon modulated by the artistry of French designers. A new art made its appearance: the art of the garden. It was Charles VIII who brought in from his Sicilian kingdom Pacello de Mercogliano, a Neapolitan religious who laid out the gardens at Amboise and Blois, with finely embroidered flower beds, sculpted shrubs and fountains and a host of other refinements.

After the end of the Valois, the Court settled in Ile-de-France, and the decline of the Loire Valley set in. The pompous equilibrium of the 17th century, as visible the Gaston d'Orléans wing of the château of Blois, replaced the graceful fantasies of the 16th. Towers became pavilions, rooms were monumental, and roofs rose in the French style. This period and style are well illustrated by Ménars and Montgeoffroy.

In the 18th century, a penchant for urban planning manifested itself: as at Orléans, Tours and Saumur, designers laid out enormous perspectives, centered on superb bridges.

Nowadays many monuments are being restored, either by generous patrons of the arts, or by the State. Old buildings are being consolidated, maintained and furnished. Many modern artists have helped in this renovation of a heritage which is one of the glories of France.

We therefore invite our readers to accompany us on a stroll through the pages of French history, along the banks of the Loire.

JANINE ET PIERRE SOISSON

SULLY

The château of Sully-sur-Loire, which was almost entirely built before 1360, is an imposing rectangular fortress with round towers at each corner. It was built at the edge of the river bank. The Guard Room on the ground floor, the large room on the first floor, the oratory and, most notably, the timberwork of the upstairs room in the keep are in an excellent state of preservation.

This timberwork is the finest that has come down to us from the Middle Ages. It was cut from chestnut wood prepared with the utmost care by the marvellous craftsmen of bygone ages: trees aged between 50 and 100 years were felled in winter, their bark having been removed first while they were still standing; they were then squared off leaving only the heart; next they were left for several years underwater in a river so as to eliminate all the sap, and finally they were covered with a layer of disinfectant. When treated in this way chestnut wood is safe from parasites of any sort; moreove the beams were assembled in such a way that the air could circulate freely. It is for these reasons that they seem so new to us today.

Sully is associated first of all with the memory of Maurice de Sully. This man of humble origins became the bishop of Paris in 1120, and it was he who drew up the plans and ordered the construction of Notre-Dame de Paris.

In 1381 the château became the property of the Trémoille family, originally from Poitiers, which had distinguished itself in the Crusades.

Early in the 15th century Sully belonged to Georges de la Trémoille, a former chamberlain of John the Bold who had become the favorite of Charles VII, thus securing for himself rank and fortune and consolidating his earlier rapacious gains. In 1429 Charles VII was living in Sully. In February an interview took place, at Chinon, between a man who was still only the King of Bourges and a little peasant girl from Lorraine, named Joan. Once her tiny force had been equipped, Joan rushed to Orléans where she joined forces with Dunois who was defending the city. The courage of the French was restored, while the English seemed paralyzed. Subsequent events were quite miraculous; one by one the bastions built by the English to block off the town fell to the attackers. On the morning of May 8 the siege was lifted. Prompted by Joan, the king immediately marched on Reims, where the young maiden intended to have him crowned, as her 'voices' had instructed her. "With both bumpkins and hardened soldiers obeying her every command", in the words of Péguy, she seized, in swift succession, Meung, Jargeau and Beaugency, clearing the path for her prince through a region full of English troops. The decisive victory of Patay finally liberated the region of the Loire routing the English relief army. Talbot, the famous English captain, was taken prisoner. Auxerre, Troyes and Chalons then opened their doors wide to the *fleur-de-lys* banners and Charles entered Reims, unopposed, and was crowned there on July 17 1429.

Thereafter the victorious period of Joan's campaings seemed over. The king was pursuing a policy of negotiation and apeasement. La Trémoille, who was jealous of Joan of Arc's fame, turned the king against her. At the beginning of 1430 she returned to Sully. In the previous few months the role played by La Trémoille had been somewhat sinister. He had plotted with the English in order to save his own property, and did not hesitate to obstruct Joan's offensives. While staying at Sully she was treated virtually as a prisoner and had to flee in order to go on fighting. In March 1430 she was captured outside Compiègne, to which the duke of Burgundy was laying siege. The rest is familiar history.

In 1602 the château was bought for 330 000 *livres* by Maximilien de Béthune, baron of Rosny, minister under Henry IV, who was to become duke of Sully in 1606.

Sully, whose name is inseparable from that of good King Henry, from plowing and grazing, a "chicken in every pot" and a whole range of golden legends, was certainly one of the greatest of all French statesmen. This valiant Protestant captain was the best artillery man of his age. He was also a remarkable administrator who, in a few years, with the confident support of the Béarnais, restored the health of France after the turmoil of half a century of civil strife.

In 1610 Henry IV was assassinated. That was the end of the career of the great minister, who had remained faithful to the Reformed Religion. Once the Catholic pro-Spanish party had returned to power he had to resign from the Council in 1611. He still served his country by trying, though unsuccessfully, to persuade the Protestants of Montauban and La Rochelle, to agree to submission; this earned him the rank of Marshal, which was offered by Cardinal de Richelieu in 1634. Living in his sumptuous retreat at Henrichemont or his château of Sully, the former companion of Henry IV wrote his *Memoirs,* in which he severely criticized the new rulers of France. He entitled them *Memories of the wise and royal economies of State of Henry the Great.* The story goes that, fearing indiscretions, he had a printing press set up in one of the château towers, and that the famous *Memoirs,* which appeared in 1638 with the name of a printer in Amsterdam, were in fact printed in Sully.

Sully embellished the château. He built earthworks to separate it from the river, and dug ditches which were to be filled by a diverted stream; he laid out the park and enlarged the buildings of a pavilion in which he later lived.

The third man whose name is associated with the château is François-Marie Arouet, a young man of 22, full of talent, who was all the rage of the Parisian salons. In 1716 Arouet had been forced to leave Paris on account of some disrespectful and critical verses against the Regent Philippe of Orléans. He stayed at the château several times, where he was the darling of the social world which the duke of Sully had assembled around him. A theater was set up in the large room on the second floor, where he staged comedies, together with some ravishingly beautiful women. This charming rake was later to be known as Voltaire.

Facing, the château of Sully (see also first page). Above, the château of Chambord.

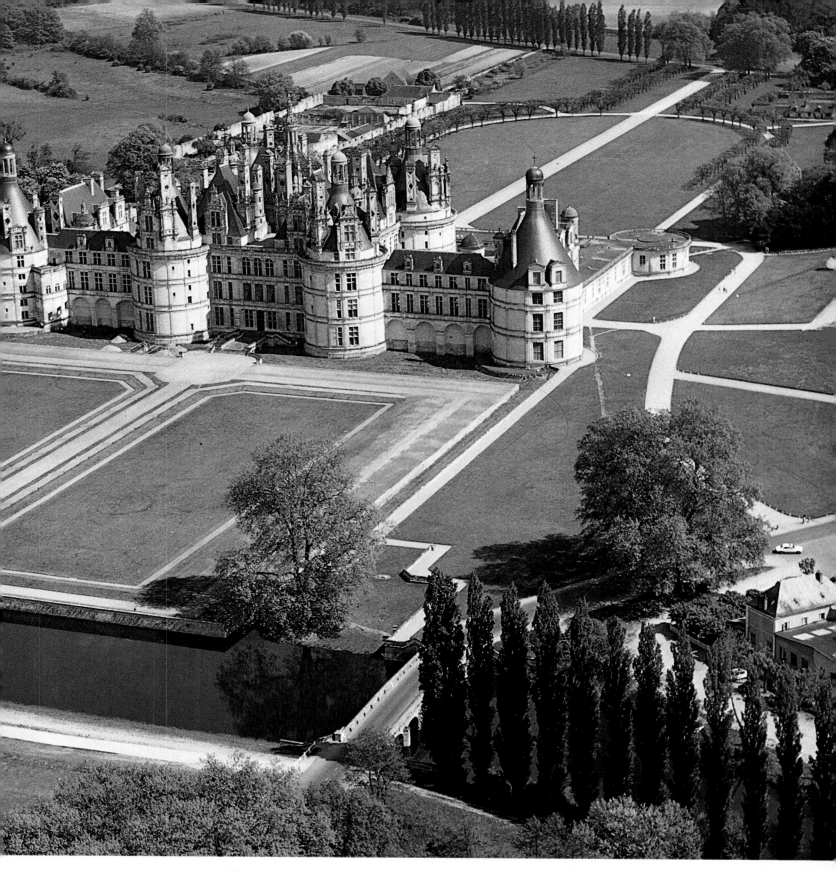

CHAMBORD

Chambord is a masterpiece. It is perhaps the best-known of all the Renaissance châteaux. It is enormous—170 yards long and 128 yards wide—and is built according to the feudal layout: a central keep with four towers, linked to the outer corner towers, on the north-west face, by two floors of galleries. The entire structure forms a gigantic white mass which suddenly comes into view around a bend in the path through the woods; one is left breathless by its splendor.

This château was a product of the will of Francis I, a lavish giant of a man who decided to build this magnificent residence—which, though conceived as a fortress, is not at all military—on the site of an old hunting lodge, in the midst of a

forest well stocked with game, 9 miles from Blois. Work proceeded at a brisk pace from 1519 onwards. The name of the architect is unknown, but the builders were Denis Sourdeau, Pierre Neveu and Jacques Coqueau. Francis I was filled with a veritable passion for this venture: so much so, that even at the worst moments of his reign, when he could not afford to pay the ransom of the sovereign's two sons, who had replaced him in his Spanish prison shortly after the defeat at Pavia ("All is lost, Madame, save honor!"), work on the château never stopped. It took more than fifty years to complete, and Francis I never saw it finished.

Starting in 1539, however, he spent as much time as possible at this more than royal residence, which he casually referred to as "my place in the

country". He was host there to Charles V, who was suitably impressed: the emperor, beset by a swarm of nymphs who scattered petals before him, was barely able to stammer: "The whole of human industry is represented here!" In the château estate Francis hunted deer and wild boar, and entertained lavishly in the château itself.

And of course Chambord seems to have been designed specially with this in mind: the park covers 13,600 acres, enclosed by a wall 20 miles long—the longest in France—and the château consists of buildings with a total of 440 rooms, a fantastic monumental staircase, and superb terraces from which the Court used to watch the spectacles arranged for its pleasure: parades, tournaments, balls, and the hunt. The terraces, which are decorated with skylights, gables,

lanterns, bell-turrets, spires, 800 capitals and 365 sculpted chimneys, are unique.

Let us now return to the staircase situated in the middle of the Guard Room. It is also unique: richly decorated in the Italian style, it consists of two spirals which are superimposed but never

meet; the central nucleus is pierced, thus making it possible to see from one spiral to the other. When first built, it rose straight to the roof without stopping. But a number of difficulties, particularly, it seems, severe drafts, made it necessary to build landings on each floor. It ends in a single spiral revolving above the terrace in a magnificent lantern nearly 100 feet high.

Under Henry II construction continued. In 1552, on his return from his journey to Germany, during which Henry II occupied Toul, Metz and Verdun, he chose Chambord as the setting in

Various views of the château of Chambord. Top left, royalty out for a stroll, in the 17th century, near the château.

which the three German princes were to sign the treaty which conferred upon the Crown the three bishoprics, in the presence of the count of Durtal, who was keely looking forward to this outcome so that he could become governor of the three towns. Louis XII often went hunting at Chambord: le was a brilliant horseman who was capable of jumping ditches 17 feet wide. Francis II and Charles IX were also frequent visitors to Chambord, where they went stag-hunting. The story goes that Charles, after spending ten hours in the saddle without a break, and exhausting five horses under him, blew so hard into his horn that he spat up blood—a strange exercise for a consumptive.

Henry III, like Henry IV, spent little time at Chambord. The truth is that, despite its lavish style, it is not very comfortable, particularly in the winter: its sheer size makes it virtually impossible to heat.

When Louis XIII, in order to rid himself of an inveterate conspirator—actually his brother Gaston d'Orléans—gave him the countship of Blois, the château of Chambord was included in the gift. Gaston, a fond father, often indulged the favorite whim of his daughter, the future Grande Demoiselle: they would go up and down the steps of the astonishing staircase, each on one of the spirals, without ever meeting. Again at Chambord, though at a later date, Anne Marie Louise d'Orléans played another game: she declared her love for the duke of Lauzun, by taking him to a mirror which she dulled by breathing on it so as to write the name of the man she loved. They married in 1681.

After the death of Gaston, Chambord reverted to the Crown. Louis XIV went there only nine times. According to tradition, it was here that Molière wrote *M. de Pourceaugnac*, in a matter of days. The comedy-ballet was performed in the presence of Louis XIV. Yet none of the script could elicit a smile from the king. The courtiers, who had often been ridiculed by Molière, were delighted. The author, the actors, and Lulli, who had composed the music and was also on stage playing the part of an apothecary, were all in a state of anguish. Suddenly, Lulli had a brilliant idea: he jumped with both feet together onto the harpsichord, which promptly collapsed. The king roared with laughter, and that saved the day.

Louis XIV was also slow to laugh during the performance of the *Bourgeois Gentilhomme*. He did not congratulate Molière until the second act —but the play was thereafter a great success.

Louis XV, who had married Maria Leczinska, lent the château to his father-in-law, who had lost his Polish throne. Stanislas lived there for a time. Then, to reward him for his brilliant victory at Fontenet, he presented the estate as a gift to the Maréchal de Saxe, together with an income of forty thousand pounds. The Maréchal moved in, in lavish style. In the outbuildings he housed two cavalry regiments consisting of Valachians, Tartars and black troops from Martinique. Their horses were imported from the Ukraine. Maurice de Saxe is responsible for the monumental ceramic stove which sits imposingly in the vestibule on the first floor. This violent despot was also a ladies' man: the château was the setting for his affair with Favart, the famous singer, for whom he had the stage on which Molière once

Chambord. Left, two views of the staircase of the château. Top right, upstairs room opening onto the staircase, and a stove brought to the château by the Maréchal de Saxe. Bottom, a painting by Gérard, one of the numerous adornments of the château; it is the Recognition of the Duke of Anjou as King of Spain. *A royal bedroom.*

Chambord. Above, the Salle des Soleils and, right, two views of the Hunting Museum. Note, at top right, a tapestry depicting King Francis I. Below, the tapestries in the dining room.

Chambord. The Royal Bedroom, the chapel and a canal in the gardens. Right, the château of Blois, inner and outer façades.

played put back in place. When he died—of a cold, or in a duel with the prince of Conti, whose wife he had seduced, depending on the version of events one believes—the cannons of the main courtyard, in keeping with his will, fired a salvo once every quarter of an hour for six days.

The château is now sparsely furnished. There are some fine tapestries in the Louis XIV apartments, and some paintings, including one magnificent portrait of Henry III by Clouet, and another of Ann of Austria by Mignard. We are also reminded of the count of Chambord: there is a stately bed presented to him by his supporters; it is near a small set of artillery pieces, a toy with which the prince amused himself during his childhood. On the ground floor there is an exhibition of carriages and harnesses made by Hermès in 1891, and which were to have been used by the Pretender on the occasion of his royal entry into the capital, which never took place: his attachment to the white flag cost him his throne. Ever since then, the trappings of a coronation which failed to happen have lain here pathetically.

In the study of Francis I, there is a window pane on which the following words are engraved: "Souvent femme varie, bien fol est qui s'y fie" (A woman is very fickle, and he who would trust her is foolish). According to tradition it was Francis who, one melancholy day, wrote this sad formula with the diamond on his finger.

And the same nostalgia is felt by today's visitor to this colossal empty monument, which is a little too big, too white and too sad.

BLOIS

Like most of the châteaux of the Loire, Blois stands on a site which is admirable from two points of view: the great beauty of the surrounding landscape and the strategic value necessary for a fortress. In other words, as was frequently the case, the old feudal fortresses which had been built centuries previously after a careful quest for suitable sites, and whose military merits had, with time, ceased to be relevant, were eventually demolished or renovated. The château of Blois, with its huge buildings arranged around a large and roughly square courtyard, provides a nice example of this phenomenon.

The county of Blois was one the bridgeheads which were so important in the Middle Ages. The château was built in the 13th century on a steep hill overlooking the Loire by the counts of Chatillon. Its medieval feudal hall is of special historical interest: it was here that the States General were to meet in 1576 and 1588. The Tour du Foix, which stands at one of the corners of the present courtyard, is also a vestige of that remote period; like the ditches and the counterscarp, it was part of the feudal walls. The present Place du Château was the feudal forecourt and was surrounded by the wall. It was her that Joan of Arc, before leaving for Orleans in 1429, had her soldiers take holy communion—after driving off the loose women who followed them everywhere.

Such was the contribution of the counts of Chatillon to this important architectural complex.

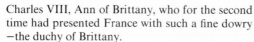

How did they come to be dispossessed? The story is one of sheer cynicism. In 1391 the count of the day was quite old, while his wife was as beautiful as she was young. She was in love with Louis d'Orléans,brother of Charles VI, the Mad King. Her love for him was such that she gave him not only her charms, and a great deal of pleasure, but also large amounts of money. So much so that Chatillon was ruined, had to sell his château to none other than the duke of Orléans, who had become newly rich by means of a shrewd transfer of funds. Fortunately for the cause of morality the duke was assassinated in Paris on orders of his cousin de Bourgogne; it was his widow, Valentine de Milan, who retired to Blois. She died there. The eldest son and heir was the charming Charles d'Orléans, one of the most delightful French medieval poets. Having been wounded at Agincourt, he spent twenty-five years in captivity in England; homesickness was a source of inspiration for his poems, as he thought back nostalgically to his childhood at Blois. His first wife, the daughter of Charles VI, had died in childbirth while he was quite young. On his return to Blois he demolished part of the château in order to build a more comfortable dwelling and, in particular, an arched gallery of which about a half is still standing today. He organized a small court for artists and writers. After remarrying twice he was blessed with the joy of fatherhood, at Blois, at the age of seventy one: his son was to be the future king of France, Louis XII, later known as the Father of the People, and who was crowned on the premature death of his cousin Charles VIII, who had died without children.

Louis XII made Blois the Versailles of the Renaissance. It was to be his favorite residence, and that of his second wife, the widow of Charles VIII, Ann of Brittany, who for the second time had presented France with such a fine dowry —the duchy of Brittany.

He thus proceeded to build a handsome two-story building of brick and stone between the feudal castle and the Tour du Foix. The façade is charming and imaginative. The great Flamboyant Gothic entrance is surmounted by an equestrian statue; the windows have lamp-standards with some rather saucy carvings. The porcupine, an emblem of Louis XII, later adopted by the town of Blois, occurs frequently as a decorative motif. On the first floor, Louis' bedroom opens on to a balcony. He was said to hold conversations, from one window to the next, with his minister, Cardinal d'Amboise, who was his immediate neighbor. The interior is richly appointed in the Italian style, with a distinct emphasis on comfort: a gallery runs the whole length of the building, thus permitting separate access to each room. This was a welcome innovation, as rooms had previously been interconnected. There are two spiral staircases at either end. The king replaced the feudal chapel by a bigger one, the Saint-Calais chapel, now partly in ruins. He built terraced gardens on the feudal forecourt, now Place Victor Hugo.

On the death of Louis XII, in 1515, Francis I, his cousin, ascended the throne. Il Baccatore, the Italian architect who was later to design the château of Chambord and the Hôtel de Ville in Paris, was still working at Blois. Francis was a lavish sovereign and patron of the arts and of literature. His wife, Claude de France, the daughter of Louis XII, was raised at Blois and remained very fond of it. Consequently the king decided to enrich the château and ordered the construction of a very large wing, adjoining the feudal castle opposite the Louis XII wing. The new structure was built backing on to the ramparts, and with plenty of windows. Although the Italian style was then very much in vogue, the new building, work on which lasted from 1515 to 1524, has many features that are evidence of purely French caprice. Symmetry is scarce or non-existent, the choice of decoration varies from one window to another, from one balcony to another, and there is an abundance of elegance and rich effects. The outer façade, known as the Façade des Loges, is a uniquely superb piece of architecture. A spiral staircase, embedded in the façade and encased in a magnificently carved octogonal stairwell, was built on the courtyard. This masterpiece had two purposes. Besides being

Blois. A window, the equestrian statue of King Louis XII over a door, the porcupine which was the king's emblem. A fireplace bearing the initials of Louis and Ann of Brittany. Facing, the bedroom of King Henri III. Right, the decor and fireplace of this room are particularly note-worthy. Following pages: a corner of Henri III's bedroom, where the Duc de Guise was assassinated the day before Christmas Eve 1588.

a means of getting to the upper floors, it also served as a kind of balcony from which the sumptuously dressed lords and ladies of the court could watch the lavish spectacles with which François I used to entertain his guests.

The poor Claude de France derived little benefit from these improvements: she died in 1624, at the age of 24, after bearing her husband seven children in eight years. The ermine, her symbol, occurs frequently in the building, sometimes accompanied by the salamander which was so dear to her husband. The first floor, which was restored by Duban, is dazzling in the brilliance of its decor—some would say it is a bit overpowering; unfortunately, however, it is unfurnished. Some very handsome fireplaces still remain. The room of Catherine de Médicis is picturesque and, like Catherine herself, disturbing and mysterious. Its 237 carved wood panels conceal hiding places and secret compartments which can be opened by pressing a pedal recessed in the plinth. Here one's imagination can run wild: what could the queen have been hiding there —poisons, jewels, State papers, sordid intrigues?

The second floor was the scene of a famous crime.

The entire history of the Valois dynasty revolves around Blois, but it was under Henry III, the third crowned grandson of Francis I, that the tragedy took place.

The States General of September 1588 had been held in the feudal hall of the counts of Chatillon. The five hundred deputies seemed to be fairly completely on the side of Henry de Guise, leader of the Catholic League, and known as Scarface. Henry III sensed that his throne was in danger, and therefore decided to do away with Henry de Guise and his brother, the cardinal of Lorraine.

On Christmas Eve 1588, at 7 am, the King's Council opened. It took place in the old chamber,in a building which has since been demolished. The giant − Henry de Guise was 6 1/2 feet tall − seemed quite relaxed as he waited for the meeting to start, although, just as he was leaving the bed of Charlotte de Sauves, his exquisite mistress "with the violet eyes", he had been handed two notes warning him of a plot against his life. However, he had dismissed them with a laugh. Now he was munching on some Brignole plums he had taken from his porcelain box. Among his faithful "45", the king had chosen 20 men, 8 of whom were in the bedroom itself while the other 12 waited in the old chamber. Montseriac struck the first blow, with the words: "Ah! traitor, you shall die!" The others all leapt on their victims and hacked him to pieces; the giant collapsed, muttering: "My God, my sins are against me. Have mercy on me!" He put his hand in his mouth and passed away.

The contented Henry then strode down the great staircase to announce to his mother, Catherine de Médicis: "I am now king of France, having killed the prince of Paris". The old lady of Florence muttered: "Let us hope to God that you have not become the king of nothing at all". She died twelve days later.

In the meantine the cardinal of Lorraine was executed in his cell, both bodies were burnt and the ashes thrown into the Loire.

With Henry III, who died childless, the branch of the Valois-Angoulême came to an end. His cousin Henry of Navarre reigned under the name of Henry IV. His wife in his second marriage was Marie de Médicis who, after the death of her husband, who was killed by Ravaillac in 1610, was an authoritarian regent. Louis XIII, his son, exiled Marie de Médicis, after the murder of Concini, Maréchal d'Ancre, her favorite, to the château of Blois.

Thereafter the prominence of Blois began to decline. When Louis XIII give it to his brother Gaston d'Orléans, count of Blois, he did so virtually in order to banish him—certainly in order to rid himself of an inveterate conspirator. The new owner found himself with a great deal of enforced leisure which he sought to occupy with building projects. Finding his resources sharply reduced by Richelieu, Mansart had to be content with the construction of the monumental but incomplete Gaston d'Orléans wing.

There is a good overall view of this side of the château and of the Façade des Loges from the small terraced garden which overlooks Place Victor Hugo. At the same place one cas see the pavilion of Ann of Brittany, which was, during the reign of Louis XII, an oratory belonging to the château gardens, where the king and queen went to pray.

Blois. Left, fireplace adorned with the emblem of Francis I, the salamander, and the bedroom of Catherine de Médicis. Right, the Council Chamber and a picture of the assassination of the Duc de Guise.

CHEVERNY

Cheverny is one of the rare châteaux of the Loire which was built in one single operation, with the same inspiration and based on the same model; it thus has a harmonious unity. Another original feature is that it was conceived as a stately home for a family which has lived in it without interruption ever since. It was built next to the old manor (1512) which was the birthplace of the future chancellor Philippe Hurault, count of Cheverny.

Starting his career as a councillor of the Parliament of Paris, and then as a close adviser of Catherine de Médicis, he became chancellor of the duke of Orléans, the future Henry III, who was to appoint him Councillor of State, then Guard of the Seals and eventually Chancellor of France. His estate at Cheverny was elevated to the status of countship—in those days a rare honor for a *noble de robe.* The count thus lived during the reigns of three kings. Having fallen foul of Henry III, he went over to the side of Henry IV, who promised to recover his post as Guard of the Seals. On his death he held the rank of governor and lieutenant general of the Orléannais, Blésois, the Pays Chartrain and the Loudunois—a distinction which was quite exceptional for a man who did not belong to the *noblesse d'épée.* He left his *Memoirs,* which were continued by his son and published in 1636, the year in which Corneille wrote *Le Cid,* and therefore a quintessentially classical year.

By then the château was completed. The architect, Boyer, who drew up the plans and the chatelaine who was in charge of construction finished their work in 1634. It is a long symmetrical building, with roofs in a classical but highly elaborate style. It is now the property of the Marquees of Vibraye, a descendant of Hurault

de Cheverny and one of the leading huntsmen in France.

The château, which is in a remarkable state of preservation, has kept its 17th-century decoration and furnishings intact. The grand drawing room on the ground floor has a selection of paintings by the Old Masters, including one canvas from the studio of Raphael showing Jeanne d'Aragon and a portrait of Marie-Johanne de Sommery by Mignard. The small drawing room is adorned with five Flemish tapestries in the style of Teniers. A majestic stone staircase, fully sculpted, leads up to the apartments.

In the guard room and the King's Bedroom there is a series of painted panels by Jean Mosnier, a Blois artist of the first half of the 17th century, which depicts the stories of Don Quixote, Ulysses, Adonis, Perseus, Theagenes and Chariclea, and, a series of five magnificent tapestries representing the labors of Ulysses, made by the Paris Looms which preceded the Gobelins.

The château is surrounded by a very large and beautiful park; the main entrance opens onto a garden in the French style. The outbuilding contains the Trophy Room with more than two thousand stags' antlers on display.

The kennel houses a pack of fifty hounds. At regular interval the Marquess organizes hunts which are reputed to be among the best in France.

The château of Cheverny; a room in the château with a view of the outbuildings. Facing, the Hunting Museum. Right, bedroom of King Louis XIII in the château.

CHAUMONT

The château of Chaumont is situated on high ground overlooking the Loire. The fortress which once stood on the site was demolished twice—the second time on the orders of Louis XI, who thereby wished to punish the owner, Pierre d'Amboise, for having belonged to the League for the Public Good.

That same year, in 1465. Pierre began the construction of the existing château, with military and strategic objectives in mind. The west wing, the oldest part of the château, has a forbidding, well-defended exterior. The windows which can be seen in it today were made later in its history. Italian influence was already in evidence and clearly softens some of the building's medieval crudeness. The other wings show the mark of Renaissance influence, their style being virtually that of the 16th century.

Charles I—the eldest son of Pierre d'Amboise, who had seventeen children—and his grandson Charles II continued and completed the château. The man responsible for the bulk of the work, Charles II, was extremely well connected. His uncle, who was born at Chaumont, was Cardinal Georges I d'Amboise, an all-powerful minister under Louis XII, who was made Legate of the Holy See to France and combined this post with that of Prime Minister. Indeed he came close to being elected pope on the death of Alexander VI Borgia. The conclave eventually passed over him, in favor of Cardinal La Rovère, who became pope with the name of Julian II. Being a good family man, the Cardinal was active on his nephew's behalf in Court: Charles became Grand Master of the King's Household, Marshal, Admiral of France and Lieutenant General in Italy. Two interwoven Cs are carved in relief on one of the façades: they are the initials of Charles II and his wife Catherine.

The carved emblem of the château's name, a mountain in flames for *chaud mont*, (hot mountain), is to be seen on another façade. The inner courtyard was originally fully enclosed. In the 18th century an owner who was fond of nature had the entire north wing demolished, thus obtaining a splendid view of the Loire. A drawbridge leads to the great main gate of the château, which bears the coat-of-arms of France and the initials of Louis XII and his wife Ann of Brittany. The entrance is flanked by two towers, one with the arms of the Cardinal d'Amboise and the other those of Charles II d'Amboise.

The château changed hands in 1560, when it was bought by Catherine de Médicis. King Henry II had died the year before, Francis II was a minor and the Queen Mother was Regent. Catherine was thus able to raise her head after years of humiliation. Such was the influence that Diane de Poitiers wielded over the the heart and mind of her royal lover that she was really only the second queen of France. Henry II died in a tragic accident in which the count of Montgomery pierced him with his lance during a jousting tournament.

The château of Chaumont, on the hills which border the slow-moving Loire. The entrance to the château and the drawbridge. Below, one of the corridors of the royal residence.

(The young lion will overcome the old/On the battlefield in a single-handed duel./In a golden cage he will gouge out his eyes,/Two classes, one only, then a cruel death.)

Less than an hour later Diane de Poitiers fell from favor. Henri had given her the delightful château of Chenonceaux, her dream house. She had devoted a great deal of effort and money to decorating it. Catherine proposed—a euphemism, perhaps, in the circumstances—to the former royal favorite that she should exchange Chenonceaux for Chaumont. Diane could only comply, and she thus abandoned the pleasant banks of the Cher for the grim walls of Chaumont.

Catherine spent very little time at Chaumont, but just enough to give the place an aura of mystery. Among those she had enlisted in her service was the famous astrologer Cosimo Ruggieri, a strange man who, like Catherine, was from Florence, and had come to France at the same time as her. She had him appointed to the abbey of Saint Mahé, in Brittanny, and had observatories built for him in several of her country houses. It is difficult to form an opinion of Ruggieri, an astrologer, scholar, charlatan and occultist who was involved in a wide range of political intrigues, even some against Catherine herself. When he was found to be implicated in the conspiracy which sent La Mole and Coconnas to the scaffold, he was sentenced to the galleys. After his release, he was accused of casting an evil spell on Henry IV and arrested again. One of the towers at Chaumont is directly linked by a staircase to Ruggieri's study, or observatory. In the words of Robert Burnant: "On certain evenings when the moon was dancing above the rooftops of Chaumont, his magic mirror made the king appear together with his sons while clearly showing the number of years they had left to live. The figures of Henry, Francis, Charles and Henry appeared once more on the glittering wall and, before vanishing, they turned around as many times as the years they were to reign..." Ruggieri's study was doubtless the setting for countless mysterious meetings between the queen and her wizard.

Catherine's own superb room, adorned with very beautiful tapestries, is a short distance away. It now contains a collection of baked clay medallions—work done at a much later date by the Italian ceramist Nini. Diane de Poitiers lived only a short time at Chaumont, where everything she saw reminded her of her more fortunate rival. She left there to live in her château at Anet, where she died. He room at Chaumont may still be seen, however, as well as her emblem, inspired by that of Diana, the ancient goddess of hunting: a horn , a bow and a quiver with her initials carved on the front of each machicolation on the ground floor.

Outside the château is a former dovecote which has been turned into a children's stable; Nini, who died at Chaumont in 1786, used it as a ceramics studio. He built a kiln which was used to produce the medallions which can now be seen in the rooms of the château. Le Ray, Governor of the Invalides, and owner of the château for part of the 18th century, persuaded the famous engraver to move to the banks of the Loire. Actually, Le Ray was involved in an excellent commercial operation: Nini used a hollow mold to make large numbers of relief reproductions of the features of notable figures of the day, and then the Governor of the Invalides made a small fortune by selling them.

At the beginning of the 19th century, Mme de Staël, finding herself ordered by Napoleon I, who had always detested her, to move to at least forty leagues outside Paris, spent some time at Chaumont before settling in her château at Coppet.

Particularly worthy of note are the magnificent stables, which were built in the second half of the 19th century and which are remarkably large and luxurious.

Chaumont. One of the bedrooms, and, right, the stables and the saddlery. Following pages: the château overlooking the Loire.

AMBOISE

The château of Amboise stands on a rocky outcrop on the left bank of the Loire. The strategic importance of its location is so obvious that one is not surprised to learn that it served as an *oppidum* in ancient times. When the bridge was built, thus providing the only dry crossing of the river in the whole region, the settlement grew. There was relentless guerrilla warfare between the counts of Amboise, who had built two fortresses on the heights, and the occupants of a third which was built on the other side of the river. The counts eventually won, but Charles VII seized their land.

His step-daughter, Charlotte of Savoy, the wife of Louis XI, preferred to reside at Amboise. Charles VIII was born and spent his childhood there. He grew very fond of the place, and in 1492 he started work on a huge château, of truly extraordinary dimensions, which he intended to be his main residence and a focal point for the arts. Italian art was just beginning to make its appearance in the kingdom, but it was in 1945, when Charles returned from his Italian campaign with large numbers of Italian artists, that he really introduced it into France on a significant scale. Il Boccador and Fra Giocondo were among the architects of Amboise. Moreover, as the king had discovered a new Eden in the gardens he had seen in Italy, he had Pacello lay out enormous flowerbeds on the terrace. On days when the king was entertaining large numbers of guests, tapestries would be attached to the four thousand hooks secured in to the walls and a huge blue veil simulating the sky was stretched out to provide protection from sun or rain. Animal fights were held from time to time; the story goes that Francis I one day had to kill with his own sword a wild boar which had charged into the royal apartments.

St Hubert's chapel was originally the queen's oratory.

This gem of the Gothic Flamboyant style was built by Flemish craftsmen on the orders of Louis XI. During 1940 military action destroyed the stained glass windows, which were replaced by modern windows by Max Ingrand depicting the life of St Louis. A remarkable lintel shows, on one side, St Christopher carrying the child Jesus and, on the other, St Hubert and his stag with the flaming cross.

The tragic and senseless death of Charles VIII occurred at Amboise. On April 7 1948, in the middle of the afternoon, he went with the queen to the handball court to watch a game. While passing through a low doorway at the entrance to the court he hit his head on the lintel. For a moment he was only dizzy from the blow, but shortly afterwards he suddenly slumped to the ground. He was carried, of all places, to the latrines where he was laid down. He stayed there until he died, about midnight.

His untimely death brought construction to a halt; however, Charles had already had time to complete numerous buildings, only parts of which now remain. These include the Royal Apartments, which were later expanded by Francis I and which are still furnished in the Gothic style and are decorated with some splendid tapestries.

Louis XII was not particularly fond of Amboise, and preferred to live at Blois. Nonetheless, he did order the construction of a wing which was completed under Francis I. Francis spent much of his youth and childhood at Amboise. He went there when he was six with his

mother Louise of Savoy and his sister Margaret of Navarre, the author of the *Heptameron,* who was renowned for her scholarship. At the time, Francis was still only duke of Angoulème; he received a refined education which made him a man of letters, an excellent sportsman and a remarkable warrior. King Louis XII, his cousin, had no male heir: "Ann of Brittany, was who was lame in one leg," writes Jean Duché, "gave him a daughter, Claude, who was lame in both legs. In May Louis XII married her to his heir, cousin Francis, a real ladies' man, and Claude thus became Queen Claude." Francis, who became king in 1515, won the victory of Marignan in that same happy year.

During the first three years of his reign, he lived at Amboise, where the court led a most enjoyable life. Indeed it was the château's Golden Age. Under Italian influence morality and taste began to affect each other. The greatest artists were attracted to France—among them Leonardo da Vinci, who spent his last years at Amboise and is buried there.

During the short reign of Francis II, "a puny prince with a foul temperament" in the words of one commentator, the château was the setting for one of the most tragic and bloody days in the history of France. It happened in the midst of a bitter religious conflict. The king was under the influence of the Guise, leaders of the Catholic party. Protestant agitators were preparing a *coup d'etat* to overthrow the Guise and bring to power

a Huguenot, the prince of Condé. The avowed leader of the conspiracy was a landed gentleman from Périgord, La Renaudie. The conspirators were to meet near Blois, where the court was situated. But a Protestant lawyer, Pierre de Quenelles, revealed the plot. Blois being a difficult place to defend, Guise had the court move to Amboise and had the king order the two principal Protestant leaders, Condé and the Admiral de Coligny, to go to Amboise. The conspirators

Views of the château of Amboise, on the banks of the Loire.

Amboise. This page: room decorated with Aubusson tapestries, vault and door of the Tour des Minimes, bedroom of Catherine de Médicis. Right, the inhabitants of the town re-enacting scenes from courtly life, in the style of the Renaissance, on one of the lawns of the château. Detail of a tapestry depicting King Charles VIII, who was to die a tragic death at Amboise. Part of the château known as the Royal Dwelling.

followed. No sooner had they arrived than they were arrested and executed. The bodies of the hanged swung from the battlements and balconies of the chateau. Members of the losing side were beheaded and hacked to pieces. Others were thrown alive inside sacks into the Loire. La Renaudie died fighting, while the prince of Condé, with a fine political sense, disowned his supporters.

Three years later, on March 1563, Catherine de Médicis and the same Condé signed the celebrated Peace of Amboise at the château. This treaty granted freedom to engage in Protestant forms of worship to the *seigneurs haut-justiciers* but allowed this only in towns under a seneschal's

jurisdiction, with the exception of Paris.

The last two Valois kings, Charles IX and Henry III, like the first Bourbon, Henry IV, hardly lived at Amboise at all. Louis XIII spent some time there hunting. When he gave Blois to his brother, the bothersome Gaston d'Orléans, Amboise belonged to the same estate. In 1631 Gaston rebelled against his brother again. By way of reprisals and also for reasons of caution, the king had all the fortifications destroyed. Once it had become Crown property once more on the death of Gaston, the château was used as a State prison: its inmates were to include Fouquet, the finance minister of Louis XIV, and the duke of Lauzun, better known in history for his amorous rather than his military conquests, who was one day to marry the Grande Demoiselle. In the 18th century, through the good graces of Louis XV, Amboise became the property of the duke of Choiseul, who played the role of prime minister. Being the property of aristocrats it passed to the state after the Revolution and remained in the hands of the State until Napoleon gave it to Roger Ducos. Its new owner was a colorful and versatile figure: as a *montagnard* deputy, he voted for the death of the king; as a member of the Council of the Elders under the Directoire he was an accomplice of Bonaparte in an attempt to overthrow that same Directoire.

The Heurtault Tower, which looks over the southern part of the château, is similar but bigger. Italian influence can be seen in the lintel over the door.

Amboise. Among the outbuildings of the château, the Clos-Lucé manor, granted by the king to Leonardo da Vinci after he had left Italy for the last time. Leonardo's bedroom, one of the rooms and a painting by Ingres showing Francis I witnessing the death of a man who was certainly one of the greatest geniuses of all time. Above, a bust of Leonardo in the château grounds.

Amboise. Window looking out onto the gardens and the Touraine landscape. The royal chapel of Saint-Hubert, its stained-glass windows and the lintel over the door.

CHENONCEAU

The most elegant, delicate and original of the châteaux of the Loire was designed by women, though its origins lay in the midst of male-dominated turmoil. In the Middle Ages there was a fortress on the bank of the Cher; like many others it was built solely for purposes of defense, with little thought for comfort or style. It was surrounded by ditches and linked to the shore by a drawbridge. The estate belonged to the Marques family, whose nobility was matched only by its lack of funds. From time to time, in order to keep its finances afloat, the family would sell off a plot of land. They never had any difficulty in finding a buyer—and it was always the same buyer, Thomas Bohier, Collector of Taxes under Charles VIII, Louis XII and Francis I.

Bohier, a rich, shrewd financier, was no philanthropist: he wanted the château. The day eventually came, in 1512, when the Marques family found itself ensnared in a genuine spider's web: all the surrounding land belonged to Bohier. For 12,500 *livres,* they had to cede the fortress.

Except for the keep, it was promptly razed. Bohier was then able to make his dream come true, and build his château. However, official business made such demands on his time that it

Two views of the château of Chenonceau and the surrounding landscape: "the most delicate and the most original of the châteaux of the Loire".

was his wife, Catherine Briçonnet, who supervised the construction. She also came from a family of financiers and was not averse to displaying her tastes and her authority. She imposed her own style on the château. The building is graceful, regular and rectangular, and is arranged around a vestibule, with triangular ogive vaulting, which is clearly the work of a thoughtful hostess since it is centrally located. Another practical innovation is the staircase, which is straight rather than spiral. On the ground floor there are four splendid rooms, and four bedrooms of the same size on the first floor. A turret is situated at each of the four corners. The initials of Thomas Bohier and Catherine (T.B.K.), occur frequently throughout the house as does their cryptic motto, *S'il vient à point, me souviendra* (probably: If this house is ever finished, it will recall my memory).

Thomas died in 1524, and his wife two years later. Francis then found that his Tax Collector was more shrewed than honest; in order to settle his debts to the Treasury, the heir had to cede the property to the Crown. The Connétable of Montmorency then moved in. He was frequently host to his sovereign, who, like him was passionately fond of hunting.

In 1547 Henri II ascended the throne. It was not his wife, Catherine de Médicis, who reigned over his heart, but the beautiful duchess of Valentinois, Diane de Poitiers. She was twenty years older than him, but she was divine. The duchess, who was the widow of an old hunchbacked husband, wore only black and white: the king eventually took to wearing the same colors. She had been the mistress of Francis I, who had asked her to instil some worldly wisdom into his robust but immature son. "You just leave it to me, I'll make him my lover", was the reply. In fact he kept that distinction until his death. And she was still divine. In the words of a contemporary admirer, "at the age of 70 she

Chenonceau. The arches over the Cher, a drawbridge, two gates. Decorative details of windows and balconies. Facing, well in front of the Tour des Marques.

is as pretty and as sweet as she had been at 30". When he ascended the throne, Henry gave her Chenonceau. She was to be the second lady of the house.

She laid out the magnificent garden east of the keep, on the right bank of the Cher. The bridge, built across the river on the piles of an old mill, was an inspired idea of hers. She commissioned Jean Goujon to execute certain decorative features of the mansion, including a superb fireplace in her bedroom.

All these things were expensive, but Diane had resources. Her royal lover granted her a large part of the 20 *livres* bell tax levied on all the towns and villages of France—a move which prompted Rabelais to write that "the King has hung all the bells in the kingdom around his mare's neck".

The third lady of Chenonceau was to be Catherine de Médicis. In keeping with the prediction of Michel de Nostradamus, the king was accidentally killed in a tournament by Montgomery. Once she had become regent, Catherine took her revenge: she forced her beautiful rival to exchange Chenonceau for Chaumont. This latter château is splendid, but rather grim. Eventually Diane moved on to her own château d'Anet, where she died.

True to the Médicis tradition, Catherine was fond of the arts and of high living. She laid out a park and had a number of outbuildings constructed. Moreover, from designs by Philibert Delorme, she had a two-floor gallery, 190 feet long, built on the existing bridge; it was decorated in the Italian style, with a black and white tiled floor, and was embellished with Carrara marble. The upper floor was to be used as a ballroom. In the château itself, she redecorated her Green Cabinet and added a number of windows on the façade, which she adorned with cariatids.

Some memorable entertaining took place there: on the occasion of the arrival of Francis II and Mary Stuart and of Charles IX, and, in particular, in honor of Henry III in 1577. Catherine was anxious to outdo the lavish party which Henry himself had given at Plessis-les-Tours, at which the women were dressed as men, and the men as women. She mobilized her celebrated flying troupe of young beauties, whose services she used in order to seduce either friend of foe, as the need arose, and gave an extravagant banquet. The king was clad in a pink and silver brocade dress, his hair sprinkled with violet and glittering with diamonds. Huge pearls hung from his ears and the cleavage of his dress was so deep that, in the

words of a contemporary observer, it was difficult to tell whether he was "a king-woman or a man-queen".

After dinner in the grounds of the château, served, we are told, by "the most beautiful and virtuous women of the Court, half-undressed", a host of nymphs emerged, similarly clad, from the woods; there after, ambiguous lovemaking continued until dawn.

After the assassination of Henry III, Chenonceau became calm once more. The Widow-Queen, Louise of Lorraine, withdrew there to live in strict seclusion, always dressed in white, the color of mourning worn by queens. For that reason she was known subsequently as the White Queen or Lady. Today the ceiling of her bedroom had been built into the center of the ceiling of the ground floor of the gallery.

Chenonceau slumbered on until 1733, when Dupin, the Farmer-General, bought it. His second wife, formerly Fontaine, became the fourth lady of Chenonceau. She imparted a new brilliance to the place by founding a famous literary salon. Jean-Jacques Rousseau was tutor to her son and later secretary to the lady of the house, spent some very pleasant years there. He tell us that he enjoyed himself very much in that beautiful place, and lived very well—so much so that he became "as fat as a monk". On account of the high esteem which the villagers had for Madame Dupin, the château was not looted during the Revolution, and the beloved old lady eventually died there in peace. She is buried in the park.

Chenonceau. Left, Catherine de Briçonnet, who built the château, shown here with a minstrel. Right, the beautiful Diane de Poitiers, who received the château as a gift from King Henry II. Below, the bedrooms of Catherine de Médicis and Diane de Poitiers (note, above the fireplace, the portrait of Catherine). Right, Diane and Henry II, from the Wax Museum.

In 1864 the sixth lady of Chenonceau arrived. Mme. Pelouze spent her life restoring the buildings, largely on the basis of Thomas Bohier's plans. She sealed off the additional windows and banished the cariatids to the park. The interior was completely redecorated.

Now the property of the Menier family, the château is remarkably well kept up. Visitors reach the château along a magnificent avenue of centuries-old plane trees. After crossing the drawbridge one comes to a terrace where the ancient keep stands.

The ground floor of the château contains the former guardroom, decorated with 16th-century tapestries, a chapel with some fine statues including a Virgin and Child carved from Carrara marble, the bedroom of Diane of Poitiers and the Green Cabinet. In the gallery, paintings by Il Primaticcio, Van Loo, Rubens, Mignard and Nattier are on display on the walls of the bedroom of François I and also in the great drawing room with its magnificent ceilings in the French style.

On the first floor visitors can see the bedroom of Gabrielle d'Estrées, the famous mistress of Henri IV, the Royal or Five Queens' Bedroom, and those of Catherine de Médicis and Charles de Vendôme, all of which are furnished and decorated with fine Gobelin tapestries.

The original copper pots are still in the kitchen, which also contains a splendid dresser.

In the Dômes building, so named from the configuration of the roof, a wax museum has been established, depicting scenes from the history of the château.

At one time there used to be a small convent of the Capucines in the loft of the château. A curious little drawbridge was raised every evening to separate the nuns from the secular occupants of the building.

Chenonceau. Left, the central vestibule. Below, portrait of Mary Stuart, in whose honor lavish festivities were laid on at the château. Right, view of the gardens; the Great Gallery.

VALENÇAY

Ever since the 12th century a most forbidding fortress had stood in the picturesque Nahon valley, on the borders of Touraine and Berry.

About 1540 the local lord, Jacques d'Estampes, had the good fortune to renew the lustre of a somewhat impecunious family name by marrying the daughter of a financier whose wealth far exceeded his social rank. This enabled him to build a new residence in keeping with his new fortune; he had the old family fortress demolished and replaced it with a sumptuous new abode. It is the centrally located square tower, known as the "Old Tower", and one wing of the present *château*. The tower is built in the style of a keep, but not of serious military purpose: it has many windows, harmless turrets and bogus machicolations. There is ample evidence here of a new taste, which was to become classicism: the large corner towers have domed roofs, rather than the pepperpot style which was customary in the 16th century. There is also a somewhat eighteenth-century air about the pilasters super-imposed on the Doric capitals of the ground floor of the entrance pavilion, the Ionic capitals of the first floor and the Corinthians of the second.

In the 17th century the owner, Dominique d'Estampes, a descendant of the builder, erected the second wing of the *château;* its roof has alternating mansards and *œils-de-bœuf* ('ox eye' rounded openings). The result was a harmonious architectural entity with imposing proportions.

Valençay did not stay in the Estampes family, but it continued to be occupied by financiers; its successive owners included several Farmers-General and, early in the 18th century, even the famous Scottish banker John Law, whose name is forever associated with one of the most spectacular bankruptcies in French history. In that same century the south wing was renovated by a M de Vilmorin.

In 1803 Valençay became the property of Charles Maurice de Talleyrand-Périgord, former bishop of Autun, former deputy to the Constituent Assembly, former chief of the constitutional clergy, former ambassador of France in London, former émigré, former foreign minister of the Directoire and former organizer of the *coup d'état* of 18 Brumaire which brought Bonaparte to power. He was then foreign minister; during his long career he was to be Grand Chamberlain of the Empire, prince of Bénévent and vice-Grand Elector—"the only vice which he lacked", in the words of Fouché. He entertained at Valençay on a lavish scale. The west wing still contains some of his furniture, while the outbuildings have been turned into a museum incorporating many historical reminders of the man whom Sacha Guitry immortalized in his famous comedy *The Lame Devil.* One day, in a fit of anger, Napoleon I upbraided him in the coarsest terms, saying "You are a piece of s... in a silk stocking." Whereupon Talleyrand, perfectly composed, bowed, murmuring under his breath but loud enough for all present to hear: "What a pity that such a great man should be so ill bred."

In 1808 Joseph Bonaparte, his brother, ascended the Iberian throne shortly after the Bayonne meeting which led to the ousting of Ferdinand VII of Spain and his son, the prince of Asturia, by Napoleon; and the deposed king was held captive at Valençay. The treaty which restored his crown was signed there five years later. His bedroom, on the first floor of the west wing, is open to visitors.

In 1829 Talleyrand bequeathed the property to his nephew.

The two façades of the château of Valençay. Facing, Talleyrand's bedroom. Right, one of the gardens.

MONTRÉSOR

The Indrois or Petite Indre is a tributary on the right bank of the Indre. Near the confluence of the Indrois and the Olivet there is a village with a fine Renaissance church and a château standing on higher ground. The first fortress to be built on this site was the work of Foulques III Nerra, The Black, count of Anjou in the 11th century.

Foulques, who was fearless, hot-headed and brutal, truly a man of primeval energy, was not content merely to fight all the lords of Brittany, Saumurois, Touraine, Perche and Maine: he also undertook three Crusades to the Holy Land to atone for his admittedly grave sins, before dying at the age of seventy.

Early in the 17th century, the château of Montrésor was associated with Claude de Bourdeille, count of Montrésor, grand-nephew of Brantôme, who, though less warlike than Foulques, was quite as dangerous. He was the favorite of Gaston of Orléans, the brother of Louis XIII, whom he incited to revolt against Richelieu. In fact he intended to have the cardinal assassinated. The plot failed. Like Louis XIII, Richelieu died a natural death. A faction among the friends of Ann of Austria, including the duke of Beaufort, the duchess of Chevreuse and our count of Montrésor formed what is known in the history books as the Cabal of the Nobles; its purpose was to keep the queen away from Mazarin, to reconcile France and Austria and to make Chateauneuf, the former Guard of the Seals, a prime minister. Mazarin

foiled the plot, Beaufort was imprisoned at Vincennes, Montrésor fled to Holland. On his return to France he was held in the Bastille for three years before being reconciled with Mazarin. He died at the abbey of Brantôme.

The château, which was much modified over the centuries, was restored in 1849 by Count Branicki, a descendant of an old Polish family. The present owners are also from the same family. The château has a fine collection of jewelry and furniture formerly owned by John Sobieski, king of Poland. The apartments are enhanced by a magnificent staircase of solid mahogany and a selection of French, Polish and Italian paintings.

The château of Montrésor and one of its towers.
Right, view of the château of Loches and, above, the keep.

LOCHES

Although it is situated in a gentle landscape, on the calm and beautiful banks of the Indre, the site on which the château of Loches stands has always had strategic significance. This fact accounts for the steady succession of fortresses and fortified settlements which have existed there over the centuries.

In the 11th century the counts of Anjou had chosen this point to build a large entrenched camp. And when their descendant Henry Plantagenet became king of England in 1154 the walls were heavily reinforced. He was the husband of Alienor of Aquitaine, the divorced wife of Louis VII of France, who had presented him with a dowry equal to half of France. With some exaggeration, perhaps, Jean Duché remarks that "This female whim led directly to a first war with England which, like the other one, lasted one hundred years". During the captivity of Richard Lionheart in Austria, Philippe Auguste negotiated with John Lackland the cession of Loches to the French Crown. On his return Richard took a very different view: it took four hours for his raiding party to force their way in and make him once again master of Loches. Ten years later, it took Philippe-Auguste a year-long siege to win it back. Loches thereupon bacame a State prison, and its walls became even thicker. Yet, despite its forbidding appearance, this was the choice made by Agnes Sorel for her residence. In the words of Jean Duché, this ravishing twenty-year-old beauty "had a round, hard neck which was a familiar sight", since she had been Fouquet's model for his famous *Bare-Breasted Virgin*. She was the favorite of Charles VII—a depressed knock-kneed forty-year-old—and indeed was the first official favorite of a king of France. She was known as the Lady of Beauté, both for her charm, which was considerable, and also because the king had given her the château of Beauté-sur-Marne. She lived in what is now called the Vieux Logis, or Old Dwelling, a structure whose design was clearly influenced more by security than comfort.

Tower. The mortal remains of this remarkable woman are no longer there.

In the 11th-century keep visitors can see the dungeon of Philippe de Commynes. Although he had been greatly honored by Louis XI and had been a member of the Regency Council during the minority of Charles VIII, this famous historian of the reigns of both monarchs sided with the noblemen who were in league against the regents Pierre and Ann of Beaujeu. He was arrested and imprisoned at Loches and then later in Paris, before being restored to favor in the eyes of Charles VIII.

In the 15th-century Round Tower which, with the Martelet, encloses the perimeter of the château, there is a torture chamber known as the Room of the Question. Above it is a high vaulted dungeon in which Cardinal de la Balue, a minister of Louis XI who betrayed his master to Charles the Bold, was confined. Tradition has it that the cardinal was kept in an iron cage which he himself had invented. Every evening, for safety's sake, the cage—known as the Maiden—was hoisted to the ceiling by pulleys.

The Martelet has several floors of underground passages and sinister dungeons. Louis XII locked up Ludovico Sforza, duke of Milan, for eight years in this place. It seems that he died the very day of his release, overcome by emotion and the brightness of the sun.

Another dungeon, slightly lower down, housed the bishops of Autun and Le Puy, who were involved in the revolt of the Connétable of Bourbon—the man who, having espoused the cause of the Emperor of Austria, said to the dying Bayard that he felt sorry for him, to which the Fearless Cavalier replied: "No, sir, it is not I who am to be pitied, but you who have betrayed your honor and your king".

John of Poitiers, count of Saint Vallier, was

Loches. Left, portrait of Agnes Sorel, known as the "Lady of Beauty", who was for many years the soul of the château. Right, the oratory of Ann of Brittany and a picture of her on a famous tapestry. Below, the Great Hall of the Royal Dwelling and, on one of the walls, an allegory.

From the terrace there is a superb view of Loches and the Indre valley. On June 3 and 5 1429, in the great hall with the fireplace, Joan of Arc begged Charles VII to march on Reims and have himself crowned king.

The beautiful Agnes wanted to be buried in the Collegiate Church of Notre-Dame-de-Loches, now the church of Saint-Ours, and she made many generous gifts to the chapter. She died in 1650 at the age of twenty-eight, and the king himself named the man who he thougt might have poisoned her: the Dauphin, the future Louis XI. After all, since he had made repeated advances to her, been unbearably rude to her, struck her and virtually forced her out of the court at Chinon and into Loches, he could well have murdered her. In keeping with her wishes, therefore, the king had her remains moved to the Collegiate Church. Once Louis XI had ascended the throne, however, the canons, in a sudden fit of dogmatic zeal, argued that the body of an avowed sinner of her caliber could not be allowed to remain in a sacred place and they asked the king to move it to the château. The king cunningly agreed... on condition that the gifts which Agnes had previously made were restored also. The canons dropped the matter immediately.

It was not until 1809 that the tomb was taken to the Agnes Sorel Tower, or the Beautiful Agnes

imprisoned in a nearby dungeon, having been implicated in the same conspiracy. He was the father of Diane of Poitiers, the future mistress of the châteaux of Chenonceaux and, later, of Chaumont. Apparently she won a pardon from her father by yielding to the advances of Francis I. However, nothing seems further from the truth. At any rate, Saint Vallier was pardoned: he learned the good news while he was already on the scaffold.

Under Charles VIII and Louis XII, the Old Dwelling was extended by the New Dwelling, which is manifestly Renaissance in style. The small oratory of Ann of Brittany is situated in this wing.

A walk around the ramparts gives one a good feeling for the impressive mass of this defensive structure.

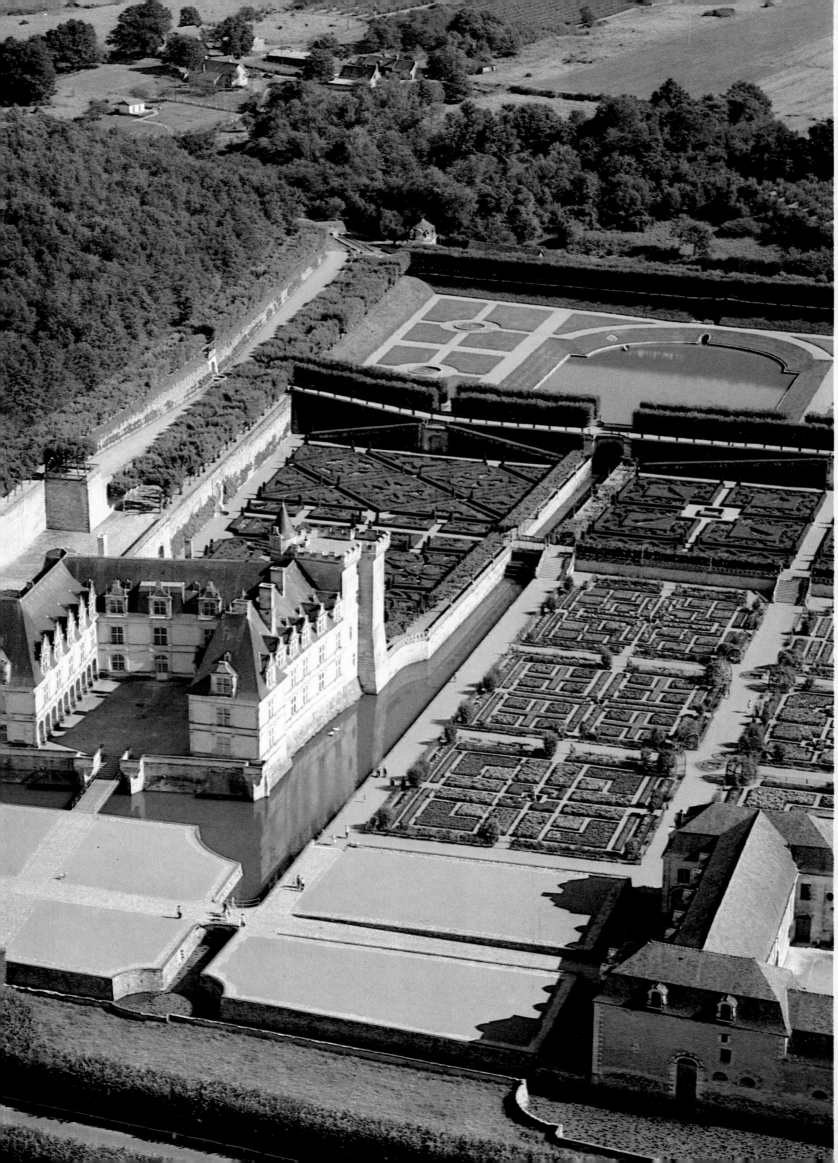

VILLANDRY

The charm of the château of Villandry and tis principal attraction lie in its gardens. It is situated in Indre-et-Loire, west of Tours; the village has a fine Romanesque church.

The present building dates from the middle of the 16th century, when it was erected on the site of a fortress, of which only a large square keep now remains, next to an old manor which, apart from some ruins behind the château, has now disappeared. The new château, which is U-shaped with a central pavillon and two L-shaped wings ending in corner pavillons was built by Jean Le Breton, a minister of Francis I.

The formal courtyard formed by these structures opens towards the Loir and Cher valley in the north. Each wing has an arcaded gallery; the lofts are lighted by large mullioned skylights.

The fame of Villandry is based, however, on its magnificent gardens, which were restored in the 19th century, according to their original design, by Dr Carvallo.

They are laid out in three tiers: water garden, ornamental garden and kitchen garden. The architectural, geometrical and symmetrical flowerbeds are framed by delicately shaped and sculpted yew and box borders, all very much in the French style. The beauty of these gardens is further enhanced by the impressive sheet of water, bordered by a stone balustrade, as well as an avenue of lindens, and elegant arbors and wall fruit trees.

Various views of the château of Villandry with its marvellous gardens. Following pages: the château of Azay-le-Rideau.

AZAY-LE-RIDEAU

The château of Azay, which stands at the water's edge, was built on a loop in the Indre.

The fortified tower which was built on the spot by Ridel, lord of Azay—hence the name of the village, Azay-le-Ridel, or le-Rideau—was destroyed in 1418 on the orders of the Dauphin, Charles, the future Charles VII, who was incensed at having been insulted by the local soldiery when passing through the region. The captain and members of the guard involved were promptly executed, and the tower no less promptly burnt down: indeed the village was known for a time a Azay-le-Brulé, or Azay the Burnt.

But these tragic memories gradually faded. A century later the royal financier Gilles Berthelot erected a new building on the same site; it is extremely graceful, even feminine—naturally enough, since construction was supervised by Dame Philippe, the wife of Gilles. The setting contributes much to its beauty. The open expanses of water, the English-style park and the great avenue of trees enhance the appearance of this early Renaissance château, making it one of

The beautiful château of Azay, like a great ship at anchor: a remarkable specimen of Renaissance architecture.

the most pleasant dwellings of its period, despite its external Gothic features. The outer walls are sculpted, the windows enriched, the turrets pointed and the machicolations perfectly fake: these refinements add much to the elegance of this quite symmetrical L-shaped structure.

Contemporary furniture, pictures and tapestries form an admirable Renaissance museum inside the château, which is thus particularly worth a visit; the straight formal staircase, a bold innovation in its day, is one of its more remarkable features.

Berthelot did not have much time to enjoy his château: he was too good a financier, and Francis I grew jealous. He had to flee, and died in exile. His property was confiscated and the château passed into the hands of different owners.

During the 1870 war the Prussians occupied it and Prince Frederick Charles of Prussia lived there for a while. In 1905 the State bought the building for 200,000 francs

Saché manor, where Balzac wrote *The Lily in the Valley*, is situated about four miles away.

All along the meandering course of the Indre, the gentle, relaxing landscape of meadows and copses is dotted with old mills and fine country houses.

Bottom of page, the outbuildings of the château of Azay. Following pages, the château of Langeais and its gardens.

LANGEAIS

Two thousand years ago the site of the present château of Langeais, on the banks of the Loire between Saumur and Tours, had been prized for its strategic importance. The Romans built a *castrum* at this point, which thereafter was increasingly fortified over the ages. The two most tireless builders of the region put their talents to work here: at the end of the 10th century, Foulques Nerra, count of Anjou, built a powerful fortress, and in the 15th Bourré, the famous minister of Louis XI, built the château which stands there today. He is in fact the same Jehan Bourré who gave his name to Plessis-Bourré, an imitation of Langeais which was built several years later.

The keep erected by Foulques, which is still

Left, the entrance to the château of Langeais, with the drawbridge over the remains of the moats. Above, façade of the château, overlooking the gardens.

standing, is perhaps the oldest in France. It saw a great deal of action, and was the prize in many battles, first between Anjou and Touraine, and then between the House of England, to which the countship of Anjou belonged, and the House of France. Philippe Auguste and Richard Lionheart were the two most illustrious protagonists of this protracted quarrel.

In 1645 Louis XI decided to erect a new building to defend against possible new attacks from the dukes of Brittany, who were frequently allied to the English during the Hundred Year's War. He doubtless remembered the War of the Two Jeannes—Jeanne de Penthièvre and Jeanne de Montfort—who, while those two houses were at their strongest, under Philippe VI de Valois, had allowed the English into Brittany. That province was still a source of great concern to the king. His son Charles VIII later solved the delicate problem by marrying Ann of Brittany, at Langeais in fact.

The strategic position of the château is truly outstanding. Standing on high ground, in the center of the town, it is a stout building in the medieval military style. Indeed it is a small fortified city designed to accomodate the local lord and his retinue, but also containing the feudal administration and the barracks for the soldiers.

Once the problem posed by Brittany had been

resolved first by the marriage of Charles VIII and Ann of Brittany, and then by Ann's second marriage, after her husband's death, with the new King Louis XII, the château, which was still royal property, was ceded to a number of men of substance for limited periods. This is one of the reasons why the building was not modified over the ages, as its various occupants were reluctant to part with their own money to improve a residence which they did not themselves own. And of course this is now seen to have been a good thing, as Langeais thus managed to preserve its purity of style.

A drawbridge leads into the château, which consists of two buildings at right angles, partly enclosing an inner courtyard. The keep which housed the garrison is an enormous round tower, flanked by two defensive towers. The seigneurial residence is a rather grim building, designed clearly with military necessity rather than comfort in mind. On the other hand, the interior of the château, which is very well furnished, conveys an accurate idea of the way a 15th-century lord lived. The external façade, facing the courtyard, is less austere. The building consists of three parts, with outer protective curtains and machicolated towers. The marriage of Charles VIII and Ann, duchess of Brittany, was celebrated in the great hall.

The Institut de France now owns this remarkable witness to the late Middle Ages, having received it as a gift from M and Mme Siegfried, who had bought it in 1886 and restored the interior with Gothic furniture and Flemish tapestries, faithfully reproducing the style in vogue when it was built. These generous benefactors were buried next to the keep, at the end of a garden laid out in the manner of the early Renaissance.

Langeais. Above, corner of the bedroom known as the Room with the Green Widowpanes and the Guard Room. Facing, tapestry decorating an entire wall of one of the bedrooms, from floor to ceiling. Right, the Blue Room, with the oldest Renaissance wardrobe.

Turning its back on the cliff, at the edge of the dark and mysterious forest of Chinon, overlooking the Indre, stands the château of the Sleeping Beauty. With its tall and bright silhouette towering above the green valley, Ussé is really like something out of a dream. The sheer volume of the château is most impressive and the number of its fortified towers gives it a distinctly unreal air; in fact visitors are often left spellbound by the sight of its array of bell-turrets, chimneys, roofs and skylights.

As was often the case, there was once an ancient fortress on the present site of the château. In the 15th century the property passed to the house of Bueil, an old Touraine family, several of whose members distinguished themselves during the Hundred Years War. There were Jean III de Bueil, his son Jean IV, master of the crossbowmen, who was killed at Agincourt, his grandson Jean V, nicknamed "the scourge of the English" campaings he took part in the reconquest of Normandy and was appointed Admiral of France in 1450. He was often involved in military action in Guyenne. Later on, however, like many other companions of Charles VII the Victorious, he fell from favor at the beginning of the reign ofmotifsXI. Together with Dunois, the bastard of Orléans, he flung himself into the League for the Public Good in an act of open rebellion. He soon returned to favor however. He left for posterity a lightly fanciful autobiography entitled *Le Jouvencel* (The Youth), which tells us much about the contemporary notion of an ideal warrior.

The château was gradually erected by these valiant soldiers. It was the quintessential medieval castle, in which gallant young men disported themselves before the courtly ladies. The rather forbidding military outer façades date from the 15th century. The far more inviting inner buildings, consisting of three residential wings, have elements of the Gothic style, but also of the Renaissance as the château was later sold by Antoine de Bueil to the house of Espinay, of Breton origin, and the new owners added their own personal touch.

The château changed hands frequently. In the 17th century the marquess of Valentinay ordered the construction of the left wing pavilion for his son, when he married the daughter of Marshal de Vauban.

Inside the château is a splendid 17th-century staircase, an antechamber adorned with a remarkable 16th-century Italian cabinet and accomodation for the sovereign, known as the King's Chamber, which may still be seen today with the original 18th-century furniture and hangings. The ground floor gallery contains a fine collection of weapons, while that on the first floor has some exceptional paintings.

Standing alone in the park is the chapel, built between 1520 and 1538, which is a pure Renaissance gem. The letters C and L, the initials of Charles d'Espinay and Lucrèce de Pons, his wife, occur frequently as decorative motifs.

According to tradition, the château d'Ussé was chosen by Perrault as a model for the setting of his charming fairy-story, *Sleeping Beauty*.

We are also reminded of Jacqueline du Bueil, comtess of Moret, a valiant fighter in her own right, who, using weapons other than those of her ancestors, was for a while the mistress of Henry IV.

In the 18th century the estate was bequeathed by Mlle d'Ussé to the Prince de Rohan, and later became the property of the duke of Duras, and then of Mme de La Rochejacquelin. It eventually came to be owned by the Blacas family, one of whose members was a minister of Louis XVIII, a very famous numismatist.

The descendants of this illustrious family are now the fortunate owners of the fairy-tale château.

On the banks of the Indre, the château of Ussé, which is thought by some to have provided the setting for the story of Sleeping Beauty. Below, a gallery in the château, a ceramic composition, the work of Luca della Robbia and a view of the gardens on the Indre.
Following pages: overall view of the château of Chinon, towering over the Vienne.

CHINON

If there ever was a place laden with history, it is Chinon. The visitor is transported at once into the Middle Ages.

The hill which looks down on the present town and the Vienne bears the ruins of three castles: the outer defensive wall of a 13th-century structure, the Fort St-Georges, the remains of the Château du Milieu, with the Clock Tower Pavilion (12th and 14th centuries), the 12th-century Tour du Trésor and the ruins of the Grand Logis (12th, 14th and 15th centuries); lastly, the Château du Coudray, with the Chapelle Saint-Martin and the Tours du Moulin, which date back to the 12th century. This entire complex of buildings is over 400 yards long and 70 wide.

The Fort St-Georges was built by Henry II Plantagenet, and is named after the patron saint of England, to whom its chapel is dedicated. Protected on three sides by the Vienne and the ravines, it is fortified more particularly in the east, the direction from which an attack would most probably come. After his death, which took place here, Henry II's body was taken to Fontevraud. The keep of Coudray was built by Philippe-Auguste. It served as a prison for the detention of a number of Knights Templar in 1308, during the reign of Philip the Fair. It is said that these soldier-monks were the authors of the graffiti which can be seen on the mezzanine. The Château du Coudray is flanked by two fine wall-towers.

Like many of the places in the vicinity, Chinon reminds us of the Hundred Years' War and Joan of Arc. The year was 1429: the English were victorious everywhere, and Orleans was under siege. The king of England had been proclaimed king of France. He and his allies from Burgundy held Paris and the greater part of the territory of France. The son of the Valois Charles VI—the Mad King—had been disowned by his mother

Isabel of Bavaria, who had pronounced him a bastard and signed the shameful Treaty of Troyes, which ceded the kingdom to the English. The Dauphin Charles, whom the Armagnac faction had proclaimed king on the death of his father, had formed an embryonic government at Bourges; he had no regular army, no financial backing and no serious allies. He is known in history as the ridiculous "King of Bourges".

On February 23 1429, at noon, accompanied by six soldiers, a young woman, almost a child, entered the town. Her name was Jehanne Darc; she claimed that, for almost a year, she had been entrusted by God, Saint Michael and Saint Catherine with the mission of saving the kingdom. She persuaded the captain in charge of the garrison at Vaucouleurs, near her village, to provide her with an escort as far as Chinon. For two days she waited, in a hostelry in a poor part of town, for the Dauphin to agree to receive her. The reception took place on the evening of February 25, in the great hall of the royal dwelling on the first floor (since the demolition of the castle on the orders of Richelieu all that remains are the first few steps and the west gable with its fireplace). According to witnesses, Joan came forward shyly. The Dauphin was hidden among three hundred notables, and one of his companions had put on his clothes. Yet the young girl did not hesitate, and went straight to Charles, who claimed not to be the sovereign. Whereupon

The above print, from the Romantic period, nicely conveys an image of the splendors of Chinon. Right: in this photograph the château seems to be emerging from the vines above the little town, surrounded by a well-wooded landscape. Facing, tapestry showing the arrival of Joan of Arc at the château: a significant day in French history.

Joan knelt down and said: "Dear Dauphin, the King of Heaven wishes to tell you, through me that you will be consecrated and crowned in the town of Reims and you will be the lieutenant of the King of Heaven who is the King of France". She assured him that he was truly the son of Charles VI, contrary to the allegations of Isabel of Bavaria, and the rightful heir to the throne. Charles, who was sorely assailed by doubts on this latter point, had a personal meeting with her, from which he emerged radiant, according to witnesses. After their meeting, Joan stayed in the keep of the Château du Coudray, on the first floor; then she was taken back to Poitiers, where she was examined by a host of matrons who were required to verify her virginity. It was felt that if she was in fact a virgin, she could not be a witch, since, as everyone knew, it was only possible to become a witch by having intercourse with the Devil. Then followed lengthy interrogations, during which prelates and theologians scrutinized the quality of her faith. Then the girl who was to be known to history as the Maid of Orleans returned to Chinon. She was given a small squad of armed men, with whom she set off on her extraordinary adventure.

The French Court remained at Chinon until 1450, after which the château slumbered until 1498, when Louis XII was host there to Cesar Borgia, the illegitimate son of Pope Alexander VI, who brought from the sovereign pontiff to the king of France the papal bull annulling his marriage to Jeanne de France, the daughter of Louis XI and sister of Charles VIII. The king was quite pleased, as the unfortunate queen was hunchbacked, lame and really ugly. Apart from anything else, he was anxious to marry the widow of his predecessor, Charles VIII, Ann of Brittany, a most worthy marital prospect who happened to possess the splendid duchy of Brittany. And so it was done.

MONTREUIL-BELLAY

Here again we have a feudal castle built by the indefatigable Foulques Nerra, count of Anjou, whose other ventures included Montrésor, Angers and Saumur. This one is perched on high ground overlooking the Thouet; it was given by Foulques to his vassal Berlay (or Bellay) I. The quarrelsome and vindictive Bellay family withstood some memorable sieges against the Plantagenets and against the kings of France. The castle was then considerably fortified with ramparts, moats, vaulted underground passages and a barbican. In 1150 the fortifications were dismantled by Geoffroy Plantagenet.

The family included Guillaume du Bellay, who was at various times a warrior, diplomat, governor of Turin and later of Piedmont. Brantôme was most impressed by his marvellous intelligence system, which enabled him to "know the secrets of almost all the princes of Europe". His brother Jean du Bellay, cardinal and diplomat, spent many years in Rome. On his first journey, in 1553, he took with him his personal doctor, François Rabelais. Twenty years later he was accompanied by his nephew Joachim, who served as his secretary. The young man, feeling homesick, wrote some touching lines on his travels:

« Plus me plaît le séjour qu'on bâti mes aïeux
Que des palais romains le front audacieux.
Plus que le marbre dur me plaît l'ardoise fine...
Et plus que l'air marin la douceur angevine... »

The imposing architecture of the château of Montreuil-Bellay and the centrally arranged hearths in its kitchens, from the Gothic period.

far prefer the house my ancestors built to the aughty palaces of Rome; and fine slate to hard arble; and the gentle climate of Anjou to the sea r).

During the 15th and 16th centuries the lords of Melun-Tancarville built new and more comfort-able residences. The château now consists of three separate parts: the oldest, as one enters, is known as Le Châtelet; then come the Petit Château and the Château Neuf. In this latter there is a fine tower with six beautifully wrought windows: it contains a staircase associated with the memory of the belligerent and Amazon-like duchess of Longueville, who one day rode up it on a horse. The walls of the oratory are adorned with frescoes on musical themes.

Below, the Gothic cellars of the château.

Montreuil-Bellay. Some parts of this feudal castle contain some very well appointed and luxurious accommodation. Above, dining room and Guard Room. Bottom left, the Bedroom of the Duchess of Longueville; below, view of the gardens and, right, the feudal lords' oratory, with 15th-century frescoes.

MONTSOREAU

The small town of Montsoreau, in the valley of Anjou, is well known for its wines, its château and... Alexandre Dumas the Elder. The ghosts of his heroine and her chivalrous lover Bussy d'Amboise roam here, together with that of the abominable lord of Montsoreau. Dumas' novel is, however, separated from the history of Montsoreau by three centuries and the whole world of difference that that implies.

The château was built in the 15th century by a member of the Chambes family. Intended partly as a residence and partly as a fortress, it has a perfect exposure: it towers over the Loire—indeed until 1820 the river used to lap at the foot of its superb but militarily severe facade. The sentry path makes a fine walk. A corner turret contains a splendid spiral staircase.

Two female members of this family were destined to play important roles. In the early years of the tyrannical reign of Louis XI, a number of disaffected feudal lords formed a League for the Public Good which brought them into direct conflict with the Crown. Their official leader was none other than the king's own brother, Charles, duke of Berry, whose mistress was a charming lady of Montsoreau. She was largely responsible for drawing him into that absurd venture which almost cost the king his throne.

It should be noted also that a lord of Chambes, a zealous Catholic, was one of the leaders of the St Bartholomew's Day Massacre.

In his *Lady of Montsoreau*, Dumas certainly took liberties with history. It was Françoise, and not Diane, de Méridor whose second marriage was to Charles de Chambes, lord of Montsoreau, Chief Huntsman of the duke of Anjou. She was charming and beautiful and he was not the mean, crafty old man of the novel. It was not at Montsoreau but at the nearby château of La Coutancière, which also belonged to the Chambes, that she met Louis de Clermont d'Amboise, lord of Bussy, and recently appointed governor of

The château of Montsoreau (15th century); here we see two views and an amusing old print of the château.

the Anjou region. According to Maurice Donnay, he had a striking presence, "handsome, with refined head, sparkling eyes, and a commanding but at the same time enchanting gaze". He was the lover of Marguerite de Valois, the sister of Henry III, who wrote that "in that century no man of his standing had anything approaching his merits, reputation, graciousness and wit". This inveterate seducer and wrangler showed himself to be quite unscrupulous and somewhat predatory in the discharge of his office. In 1579 he had fallen from favor at court, having criticized the court favorites too liberally and made many enemies. When banished to his province, he paid court to the beautiful Françoise, whose husband was absent. Did she yield to his advances? Nobody knows. Brantome and Lestoile are sure that she did. Louvet, the clerk of the Présidial of Angers, holds the opposite view. Jacques Levron finds such an idea more than doubtful.

In a manner typical of the period, Bussy wrote to a friend that "the doe of the Chief Huntsman" had fallen in his nets. Following a pattern of behavior common at the time, the friend showed the letter everywhere. Charles de Chambes heard of it. He rushed to the château, demanded an explanation from his wife who claimed she was innocent, and ordered her to write a love letter to Bussy instructing him to come and see her. She

complied. He came. Ten men were waiting for him. He struggled, but eventually died from a gunshot wound inflicted by the outraged husband.

His death attracted much publicity, but he was not missed. In his journal, Jean Louvet noted that "the death of the governor was very well received by the populace". Charles de Chambes suffered no unpleasant consequences, and the two spouses, now reconcilied, lived to a ripe old age, on the best of terms, and had at least six children.

In 1956 the interior of the château was altered to accomodate the Goums Museum, which had been moved from Rabat, as well as a number of memorabilia of Marshal Lyautey.

Montsoreau. Beams, vaults and entrance of a stairway.
Right, the towers of the château of Saumur and the same château, as depicted in the **Très Riches Heures du Duc de Berry.**

SAUMUR

On the site of the present château of Saumur, in an area, on the left bank of the Loire, which is replete with archeological remains, the counts of Blois built a fortress which the count of Anjou, Foulques III Nerra—the builder of Montrésor and Angers—captured in 1025. In 1068 it was partly destroyed by the count of Poitiers and the castle passed into the hands of the House of Anjou. It was rebuilt in the 14th century and altered in the 16th, when it was enhanced by the addition of bell turrets, skylights and gilded weathervanes. The newly enriched form of this delightful residence was compared by René of Anjou, the poet-king, to the Château of Love in his romance *Amorous heart:* "To give a fair picture of its beauty we may simply say that this fine castle was just like the castle of Saumur in Anjou, on the banks of the Loire".

At the Reformation the château was fortified by Governor Duplessis-Mornay who founded in it

a Protestant theological academy which became renowned throughout Europe. Saumur had in fact been declared a "safe place" and presented to the Huguenots by Henry III. The general assembly of the Reformed Churches of Frances was held there in 1611, after which Saumur came to be known as the "second Geneva".

The fortifications of Saumur were dismantled in 1623. The Revocation of the Edict of Nantes in 1685, followed by the suppression of the Academy, caused at least most of the population to emigrate.

Prosperity returned in the 18th century; Choiseul transferred to Saumur the cavalry school of La Flèche, the only one of the five schools founded in 1764 still in existence.

The château, which was once the residence of the governors of Saumur, now houses the Municipal Museum and the New International Museum of Horses and Riding.

It should be noted that when German forces overran France in 1940, the cadets of the Saumur Military Academy distinguished themselves by their tragic but heroic resistance to an enemy force which outnumbered and outgunned them by a very considerable margin. Their heroism was not the least of the remarkable episodes in the history of this ancient city.

Saumur. The Château, facing the Loire, and the Renaissance Room. Right, the Château of Montgeoffroy and... the impressive array of utensils in its kitchens.

MONTGEOFFROY

Montgeoffroy is a beautiful and well-ordered architectural complex, consisting of a large structure built in 1772 by Nicolas Barré, a Parisian architect who had the excellent idea of including in it the chapel and the two round, flattened towers of an earlier castle which had stood on the same site. He crowned the building with high state roofs and pink brick chimneys.

This château had the good fortune to have been owned throughout by the same family that built it so that nobody has ever tried to "improve" or modernize it. It has been remarkably kept up and is strikingly furnished with pieces by Gourdin, Blanchard, Garnier and Durand, and beautifully decorated with original paintings by Poussin,

Rigaud and Van Loo; it therefore provides us with an accurate picture of the interior of an aristocratic dwelling under the Ancien Régime.

It was built by Marshal de Contades, who was made a duke in 1789. Having begun his service as an ensign in the Gardes Françaises, he became a marshal in 1758, he died in 1793, the dean of the marshals of France.

His heirs are still the owners of the château.

On high ground half surrounded by the Aubance, not far from Angers, the famous castle-builder Foulques Nerra, count of Anjou, built a fortress whose owners, all of them fierce warriors, followed each other in swift succession until 1434.

The castle was then acquired by Pierre de Brézé, a minister of Charles VII and then of Louis XI, who replaced it with what must have been a vast and forbidding structure, all that remains of which is two round machicolated towers in the Gothic style.

On 26 May 1502, René de Cossé bought the fiefdom of Brisssac, and since then the château has been the property of that same family. In 1606 Charles de Cossé-Brissac—a Marshal of France who in 1611 became a duke and peer of the realm—decided to have the famous architect Jacques Corbineau build a new residence, an ambitious structure with seven or eight floors which would have been a great novelty for its period. The death of Charles caused the suspension of the project, and the château

remained unfinished. The present duke of Brissac defines it thus: "It is a half-built new château in a half-destroyed old château"—a fact which accounts for its lack of symmetry.

This richly decorated Renaissance structure was greatly influenced by Italian art. It is an excellent state of preservation. Situated in the midst of a magnificent park, the château was furnished and decorated with the utmost attention to detail by succeeding generations of occupants. A great gilded drawing room is adorned with an 18th-century Gobelins tapestry and a monumental fireplace; among the family's superb possessions are an outstanding Louis XIII staircase, a Gothic chapel in the 15th-century tower, a guardroom one hundred feet long, paintings by the Old Masters, tapestries and original furniture by renowned craftsmen. This was clearly a noble family which had a very definite view of French culture.

The château of Brissac, its dining room and Judith's Room. Right, the Guard Room and a picture of the reconciliation of Louis XIII with his mother Marie de Médicis, which took place in that same room in 1620.

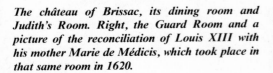

ANGERS

In the heart of an area well endowed with game and intersected by rivers containing an abundance of fish, on the Maine, an old Gaulish city stubbornly resisted the Roman onslaught. In the 9th century Aners had to fight the Normans. But it was the family of the Counts Foulques that gave the town and the château which it built nearby its true luster. Of all the members of his family, Foulques III Nerra was a particularly avid builder, those hand is to be found, *inter alia*, at Montrésor and Saumur. Under Saint Louis the Foulques fortress was built of schist and light-colored stone, on two floors; its seventeen tall and thick towers were crowned with pepper-pot roofs.

In the 14th and 15th centuries the dukes of Anjou continually added embellishments to the château. The first duke, Louis I, brother of Charles V, adorned it with the celebrated tapestry of the Apocalypse which we shall refer to later. Louis II and his wife Yolande of Aragon built the

Gothic chapel. Their son, Good King René, built a delightful and comfortable residence where he gave sophisticated parties, for which he imported peacocks, red partridges, carnations from Provence, nutmeg and several other things which had never been seen in Anjou before.

During the wars of religion, Henry III ordered the demolition of the château; but the governor, who was less than enthusiastic about the idea, proceeded very slowly, and merely lopped the heads off the towers. When Henry IV came to power the destruction promptly ceased.

This small château, which was damaged by air raids in 1944, contains a rich and unique collection of tapestries. A special building houses the Apocalypse Tapestry. This very faithful interpretation of St John's text reproduces miniatures chosen from two manuscripts, now in the library at Cambrai and the National Library which belonged to the collection of King Charles V the Wise, who lent them to his brother so that Hennequin de Bruges, his painter, could transpose the illuminations in them. In April 1377 the cartoons were delivered to the weaver Nicola

The château of Angers, in the heart of the town with its entrance and gardens. Above, the statue of King René, who used to entertain in a most refined style at the château.

Bataille, who almost completed the tapestries before his death. Originally this masterpiece comprised ninety pieces and measured 440 ft by 16 ft. Unfortunately King René presented the work to the local diocese, which failed to take the proper care of the fabric. Mishap followed mishap, and all that now remains of the Apocalypse Tapestry is sixty-nine panels and nine fragments whose overall dimensions are 305 ft by 13.5 ft.

Angers. An outbuilding of the château, known as Le Châtelet. Right and below, two details from the marvelous tapestries in the château.

Angers. The famous Apocalypse Tapestry. Below, view of the moats. Right, one of the entrances to the château of Serrant.

Serrant. The dining room. Below, an entrance, a polychrome low-relief sculpture in the chapel. Right, tapestries in the library and the bedroom of the present owners of the château.

SERRANT

A mile and a quarter northeast of Saint-Georges-sur-Loire, the château of Serrant—a stern, symmetrical and sumptuous residence—stands reflected in the deep, water of its moats.

Its construction was spread over three centuries, the 16th, 17th and 18th. The surprising thing about it is, nonetheless, its remarkable unity. Moreover, its large round towers topped by domes and the brown schist and contrasting white tufa of which it is built give it considerable character.

The plans were drawn up by Philibert Delorme in the 16th century. Building started in 1546, under Charles Le Brie; in 1596 it was bought by Hercule de Rohan, duke of Montbazon. In 1636 it was acquired by Guillaume de Bautru, later count of Serrant; this remarkable man, who had been councillor of the Parliament of Rouen at the age of 22, master of ceremonies at court, administrator of Touraine, councillor of State, frequently ambassador or *chargé d'affaires,* and a member of the French Academy, was long renowned for his sarcastic wit. His grand-daughter married the marquess of Vaubrun, lieutenant general of the king's armies, who was killed in the company of Turennes at the battle of Altenheim, on 27 July 1675. After his death, the marchioness commissiond Jules Hardouin-Mansart, great-nephew of the famous Mansart, and the architect of the chapel and the Galerie des Glaces at Versailles, to build a superb chapel in memory of her husband. She also had Coysevox build a mausoleum of white marble.

In the 18th century Serrant became the property of Antoine Walsh, an Irish nobleman, a supporter of the Stuarts, who took refuge in

France and took the title of count of Serrant.

In 1830 the château passed by marriage to the duke of Tremoille, an ancestor of Prince Jean-Charles de Ligne, the present owner.

The building is in a remarkable state of preservation and its rooms are very well furnished. The dining room is adorned with splendid Flemish tapestries. The great staircase and the coffered ceilings of the first floor are most admirable. The library contains more than twelve thousand volumes. The rooms of the château are adorned with many works of art: paintings by the Old Masters, tapestries from Brussels, fine busts of the Empress Maris-Louise by Canova, and a very beautiful Italian closet.

LE PLESSIS-BOURRE

Construction of the château of Plessis-Bourré started in 1468, about twelve miles from Angers. The building was commissioned, and work on it supervised, by Jehan Bourré, Financial Secretary and Treasurer of France under Louis XI, who based its design on that of the château of Langeais. It was completed within four years. The fact that it was built all at the same time—a rarity in the Loire valley—means that its unity is perfect. Its style, however, is transitional: it is no longer merely a feudal castle, but it is not yet a country residence; it is not really in the Italian style, though Italian influence is evident; and it is no longer the 15th century, while not quite managing to be fully Renaissance.

It appears as an enormous fortress with extremely thick walls, surrounded by broad moats, with a bridge 130 feet long, protected by a small fort with a double drawbridge; it is flanked by four towers, the biggest of which has battlements and served as a keep. A platform ten feet wide at the base of the perimeter wall provided for a broad sweep of artillery fire. Once one passes through the entrance archway, however, one finds a much more congenial kind of architecture: a vast inner courtyard, an arcaded gallery, high dormer windows (still slightly narrow, in keeping

The curious exterior of the château of Plessis-Bourré. Right, a 15th-century ceiling, decorated in a manner unique in France; detail from the ceiling: **The Indecent Fountain.** *Bottom, tapestries on biblical themes.*
Following pages: the Porte des Tourelles, in the château of Lude.

with their period), and turret staircases.

St Anne's chapel, with its slender belfry and the Hall of Justice are situated on the ground floor, just before a number of formal State Rooms which are remarkably well furnished.

On the first floor, the guardroom has a superb paneled wooden ceiling, painted in the late 15th century. A number of realistic and allegorical figures are shown: Fortune and Truth, Lust and Chastity (in the form of a unicorn) and the Musician Ass. There are also some humorous scenes such as a man trying to wring the neck of an eel, a clumsy barber at work on a patient, and a woman sewing up a chicken's crop. Here we find, after two whole centuries, the inspiration of the *Roman de la Rose* as well as that of the *Roman de Renart*.

The library contains an interesting collection of fans.

Shades of Louis XI, Anne and Pierre de Beaujeu and Charles VIII, former occupants of the château, wander between these walls which are imbued with a sense of the final decline of the medieval world.

LE LUDE

In the 11th century the *Castellum Lusdi,* an ancient fortified site, belonged to the counts of Anjou. In the 13th century, a fortress flanked by six towers was to be built right next to it. In 1378 it became the property of the Vendôme family. The English took it in 1419, but it was reconquered in 1427 by Gilles de Rais, the famous companion-in-arms of Joan of Arc, who, after serving as Marshal of France for a time, ended his days on the scaffold for causing the deaths of between 140 and 300 children while dabbling in black magic. It has often been asserted, but wrongly, that he was the basis for the legend of Bluebeard.

In 1477 Jean II de Daillon, who was born at Bourges, but whose family was originally from Normandy, bought the fief of Le Lude. Although he had once been a childhood friend of the Dauphin, the future Louis XI, he abandoned him during his quarrel with his father, Charles VII, and went over to the old man's cause. Once he had ascended the throne, Louis XI did not forget this act of treachery, and was determined to exact vengeance. In order to flee from the royal wrath, Jean de Daillon had to hide for seven years in a cave in the Maulne Valley.

He was eventually restored to favor, and became chamberlain of Louis XI; he died while Governor of Le Dauphiné, having previously held the same post in Artois. In the meanwhile he had begun to transform the old fortress into a luxurious country house. The plans of the new residence were the work of the architect Gendrot: three buildings surrounding a central courtyard, with an arcaded gallery on the side of the entrance; the former moats were turned into gardens.

His son Jacques continued with the construction of the château, building the right wing, named after Louis XII, the façade of which is adorned with an equestrian statue of Jean II. Jacques, who was a counsellor of Louis XII and Francis I, distinguished himself during the Italian wars: Brantôme mentions him as one of the "great French captains".

His heir was to complete the Francis I wing, which looks out over the park. It is a strange building: despite its Gothic features, including curtain walls and machicolated towers, it still manages to be fairly typical of the Renaissance, having windows adorned with pilasters, skylights crowned by pediments and a number of sculpted medallions.

The last member of the Daillon family, for whom the area of Le Lude had been elevated to the status of duchy, died in 1685. He was the Grand Master of the Artillery of France.

The château was altered several times. A Louis XVI wing looks out over the Loir; it is built of tufa, and has sober and well-balanced lines, with a central pediment.

In winter the huge Banqueting Hall in the Louis XII wing, which has been restored in the styles of the 15th and 16th centuries, is the setting for rehearsals of the theatrical presentation of Le Lude. A magnificent library occupies part of the Francis I wing. In the dining room, with its enormous walls, a monumental fireplace bears the symbols of Francis I and Claude de France: the salamander and the ermine.

The château of Lude reflected in the Loir. Top, the dining room and the great staircase.

CHATEAUDUN

The château consists of two parts placed at right angles. It incorporates an assortment of styles, from the 12th to the 16th centuries. In the inner courtyard, facing west and north, there are two dwellings from the late Middle Ages and early Renaissance which are flanked by lattice-work stairways. The imposing hulk of an enormous keep stands to the south. This vestige of a 12th-century fortress is one of the oldest round keeps in existence; moreover, standing 95 feet high, it is a masterpiece of 15-century structural technique. A door just over 30 feet above the ground leads to the 15th-century Sainte Chapelle, which was built for Dunois. It contains some tall Gothic statues, twelve of which are colored.

Until the end of the 17th century the château remained the property of the Orléans-Longueville family, the direct descendants of Dunois. In the 18th century, however, it fell into the hands of a commoner, the financier Dodun, a man of modest birth who was appointed Controller of Finance under the Regency.

It is worth noting the heroic defense put up by the town of Chateaudun in October 1870 against the Prussians. The Dunois—the inhabitants of Chateaudun— were outnumbered and outgunned 12 to 1 in a fierce bombardment. Once the city had been taken, the enemy set fire to it. Hence the motto later adopted by Chateaudun: *Exstincta Revivisco*, or, roughly, "I am reborn from my ashes".

The inner courtyard of the château of Château-dun. Right, one of the towers and the central part of the Longueville Wing.
Last page, at the edge of a wood in Touraine, a general view of the splendid château of Ussé and its gardens.

Designed and produced
by Editions Minerva S.A., Genève
© Editions Minerva S.A., Genève, 1981

Printed in Italy